Awed By His Grace

Out of the Bunkhouse

RANDY CLARK

Apostolic Network of Global Awakening
1451 Clark Street
Mechanicsburg, PA 17055

1-866-AWAKENING

www.globalawakening.com

Global Awakening
{ # Core Message Series }

It is our desire to bring the messages of the Kingdom to the people of God. We have taken what we consider to be core messages from Randy Clark's sermons and schools and printed some of them in booklet form. We hope this teaching increases your understanding of God's purposes for the times we are in and that you find yourself encouraged in your faith. Other core messages are available and they are listed at the end of this booklet.

Table of Contents

{ Awed By His Grace }

Amazing grace—there's so much more to God's grace than we can understand. John Newton, former slave trader and author of the hymn "Amazing Grace," understood it. He knew he was a wretch, knew he was blind, but that God had saved him and given him new eyes to see. Martin Luther got it, too. And we need to understand it more deeply—both emotionally and intellectually.

Justice is when you get what you do deserve. Grace is getting something good that you don't deserve.

Sometimes I think we look at grace through wax paper. We can see—kind of. But we haven't gotten a full revelation of how deep God's grace is for us. All too often we talk about grace, but we're unwilling to extend that grace to anyone who makes a mistake. We're quick to say that if anyone does anything wrong, that proves that what they're doing and saying couldn't be from God. In fact, all it proves is that God's grace is greater than we think.

Faith Not Diminished by Sin

I read the story of A.A. Allen's "Only Believe", by Don Stewart (Don and R.W. Shambach were the two main spiritual sons of A.A. Allen). Allen received a great anointing, but he also had a great weakness. Throughout his life, this man of God struggled with drinking. It's true, he never condoned it, and he never said it was right, but he was an alcoholic before he could walk. His mother put whiskey and wine in his bottles instead of milk. So, he got off to a bad start. Sometimes people have such brokenness, and yet God is calling them. There is strength and weakness there.

In the time before civil rights law, A.A. Allen wouldn't do a meeting if it was segregated, even in the South when they insisted on segregation. There were a lot of good things in his ministry, a lot of good people who worked for him. But he was very insecure. R.W. Shambach and some of the other spiritual sons became more powerful, he became more and more depressed and felt like he wasn't needed anymore. Then out of his depression, not fully understanding grace, he died from an overdose of alcohol. Some say that's not true, but one of his sons found the bottles and cleaned them up.

How can God allow that to happen? There were a few times that A.A. Allen ministered in power even when he was a little bit tipsy. That doesn't make sense to most of us. Yet Mark 16:17 says, "These signs shall follow them that believe." It is not the man; it's the message the man has given. It's the faith the person moves in—even though they have fallen, though they may not be right with God, if they know and trust God, the signs follow them.

This is why you can't let the charisma of a person cause you to believe in the character of the person. What's important is the faith the person moves in. And the word itself is faithful to teach the word. So if you're telling the truth about the gospel of the Kingdom, the angels are to watch over the word and bring it to pass.

This is what is so dangerous for each of us. Because if you have faith, you know the word and you are giving the word, but you're beginning to fall into some sin, you may mistake the "signs that follow" for God's approval. You think, "Wait a minute, God must approve because He's still anointing me." No, He's anointing the word you're giving. That's why it's really important to know that God's spirit, and the angels of the Lord, will honor the word when it is preached. People can lose their personal sense of intimacy with God and yet move in power out of faith. That's a dangerous thing. That's why some people have assumed God approved of what they were doing when He didn't approve. Failure to understand what was happening caused them to fall.

God's Choice

Why does God choose people? Often the ones He chooses are not the ones we would choose. God looks at things differently.

When I was a pastor in St. Louis, I met weekly with a group of six to eight pastors to pray and talk. Then Toronto happened. One of the other pastors had a much bigger church than I did. He said to me, "I don't get it. I don't understand why God would use you. I know the Bible better than you do. I'm a better preacher than you are. I'm a better teacher than you are, and I can pray better than you can. So I don't know why God would use you instead of me." And I said, "Because I'm more qualified than you are." He looked at me, and I said, "Don't you remember the passage where God chose the foolish things and the weak things to confound the wise and the strong. I'm just more qualified. I'm more foolish and not as wise as you are." And, you know, he didn't know what to say after that!

I was a little pastor in an unknown place with a little church of 50 people when I met John Wimber. God spoke audibly to him that I would go around the world and lay my hands on pastors and leaders for stirring up the gifts and imparting the Spirit. The first time I met John, he gave me a wonderful prophecy—he said I was a prince in the Kingdom of God, but I didn't have any idea what that meant. But that would be just like God—to call a Baptist preacher to impart the gifts of the Spirit. I couldn't see what was ahead, but God revealed that to others who spoke to me and encouraged me.

Reconciliation not Condemnation

As Christians, we are called to draw closer to God and to call others closer—not to condemn them for their sins, but to reconcile them with God. Here's what the word says:

> II Corinthians 5:16-21 (NIV)

> So from now on we regard no one from a worldly point of view. Though we once regarded Christ in this way, we do so no longer. Therefore, if anyone is in Christ he is a new creation; the old has gone, the new has come! All this is from God, who reconciled us to himself through Christ and gave us the ministry of reconciliation: that God was reconciling the world to himself in Christ, not counting men's sins against them. And he has committed to us the message of reconciliation. We are therefore Christ's ambassadors, as though God were making his appeal through us. We implore you on Christ's behalf: Be reconciled to God. God made him who had no sin to be sin for us, so that in him we might become the righteousness of God.

He's given us the message of reconciliation. Some people think He's given us the message of condemnation, but really we are ambassadors and our message is "Be reconciled to God." It's already been made possible through what Jesus did.

Now, I'm so glad I'm a representative of this dispensation of the gospel and not the dispensation of the law prior to the New Testament and the new covenant that was initiated through Jesus' work at the cross, resurrection and ascension. But, if we go back to the other dispensation, you read a verse like this: Deuteronomy 23:2, "No one of illegitimate birth may enter the Lord's assembly. None of his descendants, even to the 10th generation, may enter the Lord's assembly." The Old Testament's job was to help us know what sin is and the danger of it. Don't touch the unclean thing.

Grace is Greater

The New Testament shows us the greater power of grace over sin. We see Jesus touching the leper, someone unclean; Jesus speaking with the woman at the well who had been married five times and was now living in sin; and Jesus forgiving the woman caught in adultery. (But not the man — where was he?) In every case, Jesus moved beyond the law to extend grace to sinners.

Through the law we understand how much we need grace. If you don't know you're drowning, you don't appreciate a life jacket. Only when you realize "I'm in over my head, and I'm about to go under, and I don't have any strength to go on anymore" do you value the life jacket. And so the law becomes the backdrop by which we recognize we're drowning, so that we can appreciate grace.

Let me tell you a true story of God's grace. There was a woman who had been raised in a Christian home, but she had run away from God. She started playing guitar in dance joints where she met this guy and fell in love with him, but he was married. He was an alcoholic, a wife-beater and a womanizer. Despite all that, she got pregnant by him, and then two months before she had the baby, he got a divorce and married her.

After that, the woman met the Lord. She got saved. Shortly after she was saved, she heard the audible voice of God tell her to go into the other bedroom in the cheap little house they shared. It was just 10 feet to the other bedroom, but she didn't question God. She had childlike faith, and she went into the bedroom and said, "I'm here now." She felt a hot hand go down on her throat, and the big goiter she had vanished instantly.

Now, you would think that would be enough to get hold of her husband, but it wasn't. Keep that family in mind.

Let me tell you about another family. The father had run away from God, and he was the oldest guy in his county to get drafted in World War II. When he was 39, he was sent to the Pacific in the Navy. He was a sinner, and he cussed like a sailor. While he was gone, his wife was unfaithful to him, having affair after affair after affair. And he was equally unfaithful to her. The marriage stayed together, but it had begun on the wrong foot as well—with the first son born seven months after the wedding.

Both the daughter born to the first family and the son born to the second family were carried in shame in a small rural village. The daughter went to church with her Christian mother, but the son born to the other family never did. These two found each other and fell in love—and a pregnancy resulted, and the marriage came after. So another baby was carried in guilt and shame—a generational thing.

In each of these families, the child who was illegitimate was unable to form close relationships with the parents, even though other children born in these families—after the marriages—established close ties. The last little boy was never able to receive hugs or kisses from his mother or let her hold him, and he couldn't understand it. Why? Because the law says if you are conceived outside marriage, you can't be in the assembly of God. You can't enter in. You're unclean. You can't come near to God. That's under the old covenant.

That's why I love the new covenant. Because I was the little boy born from the illegitimate union between parents who both were carried in shame as well. That was me. That was my family—my mom, dad and grandparents. I learned about shame and God's grace for those conceived in sin when I was leading the revival in Toronto in 1994, and John and Carol Arnott took me through inner healing. And that's why I love grace.

God Steps In

When I was two years old, something caused my wife-beating, womanizing alcoholic grandfather and my cussing father to go to a revival meeting at a Baptist church. At a little country church with a mourner's bench, they both came forward at that revival. My dad and my maternal grandpa got saved on the same night. (By the way, I led my paternal grandparents to the Lord in 1975.)

Even though I don't remember my grandfather as the alcoholic he was for most of his life, I do know that I understood the danger of alcohol from a mother who'd grown up watching her own mother hide behind the door when granddad would come home drunk and mean. My mother had these horrible memories of growing up in an alcoholic home. Because of all she'd told me, I was so fearful of alcohol that even when I was backslidden at 18, I wouldn't touch that. Didn't even want to open that can. But I don't remember that man my mother told me about. You see, I remember another man.

I remember Grandpa Ray crying during the preaching because he who has been forgiven of much, loves much. He was remembering the man he used to be—a man I didn't even know about until I was an adult.

I also remember a man in a little bitty Baptist church. We had a pot-belly stove in the back with a row of pews on each side and four pews in the middle with a pulpit in front. We had a men's side and a women's side with an "amen" corner and a "shouting corner. Shouting women and amening men. But I liked it best when the spirit of God fell. Do you know why? Because my dad couldn't say, "I love you" unless the Holy Spirit was on him. My dad couldn't hug me or any of the kids unless he came under the Holy Spirit. But when he came under the Holy Spirit, he began to cry and he'd hug us, and he'd say, "I love you, I love you." So, I loved it when the Holy Spirit came, because that's the only time my dad could tell me he loved me. Unless he was under the influence of the Spirit, he had too many problems, and he didn't know how to do it.

Old-Fashioned Salvation

Grandpa Ray got saved the old-fashioned way. He was taught to lay everything on the altar. In those days, people were told to confess every sin they could think of and then to just say, "God, anything I'm forgetting, I confess it."

You would repent of every sin. And you'd know when you'd prayed through, because when you'd prayed through, you wouldn't feel guilty anymore. You'd know you'd been saved because the glory of God would come upon you, the spirit of God would come in you. You'd have that internal witness that the guilt was gone, the burden was lifted, and you'd prayed through, and you'd been born again.

And some men would stay at the altar night after night because they didn't feel that they had that internal witness. My pastor was that way. He went 10 times to the altar. Then one night, at home in his bedroom, combing his hair, he got the revelation, "You are forgiven!" He was overcome right there in the bedroom when it happened, when it hit him. "Well, I am forgiven!"

Once my grandfather was saved, he was a completely different man. He never touched another drop of whiskey or alcohol of any kind for the rest of his life. He never touched another woman in unfaithfulness, and he never touched my grandmother again in anger. I knew him as this gentle man that would take in other kids that had been thrown out and raise them as his own. I knew him as this humble, crying Baptist layman that just loved Jesus. So, he'd be over here crying, and over there would be grandma and my mom with their hankies going down the aisle going, "Whooooooo, whooooooo, whooooooooo." So I grew up with a shouting mom and grandma.

That's why when John Wimber asked me how come I got along so well with Charismatics and Pentecostals, I said, "because I grew up Bapti-costal!" We had everything but tongues. And that's true. There were words of knowledge and prophecy—they just didn't call it that. People just said they had heard from the Lord.

Grace for Backsliders and Hypocrites

Now, I got saved at 16 and became a hypocrite at 18. I didn't say backslid, I said became a hypocrite. A hypocrite is a backslider that is still in church.

Actually, I was a double hypocrite. At 18 years old, I got involved with the wrong stuff, doing the wrong things. I became a prodigal son. I went to the far-off country, but I stayed connected to church three times a week. Why? Because I was afraid if I got too far out in the far country, I might not be able to make it back. And, I never intended to stay out there; I just wanted to play out there for awhile and see what it was like. But I knew in my heart that I wanted to come back eventually, and that's why I stayed in the church, so I didn't get so far out.

But it got really, really bad. It got to the point that I was doing drugs every day with my two best friends. One of them was getting drunk every day and stoned every night with me. And I was doing other things that were wrong. I don't want to go into it because I don't want to give the enemy any glory here. It really messed with me. When you start doing things that are wrong, you open up Pandora's box to temptations you didn't have before. And you have hooks in you from the enemy. You sow the wind; you reap the whirlwind.

So I was a hypocrite for 11 months, a hypocrite backslider, sitting in church with my family and doing drugs with my friends. One day in 1970, I was driving around with my friends, and they said, "What do you want to do when you get out of high school?" because graduation was coming up. One of them said, "I want to go to Canada" (because the Vietnam war was going on). Another said, "Yeah, I want to have all the drugs I want." Still another said, "I want all the women I want." They came to me, and they asked, "Clark, what do you want?"

I couldn't believe what came out of my mouth! From out of my heart my mouth was speaking! It betrayed me in front of my friends. I said, "I'd like to be a preacher." Then I was thinking, where in the world did that come from? I was so embarrassed that I had said that. And they looked at me and said, "You, what?" I said, "I don't know. I didn't mean to say that."

Shortly after that, the Lord set up a divine appointment. In those days, there was nothing to do in small towns and in our town there was nothing to do except race cars. That was it…nothing else. No pool hall, no bowling alley, no theater, nothing…just race cars and drive around that place…all night. So, I was driving, playing Steppenwolf as loud as the music would go, listening to God's name being taken in vain in "The Pusher Man." A guy that I looked up to, a Holiness guy who had a healing gift, saw me. He went to my mom's house and didn't betray me, but just said, "Tell Randy I saw him last night at Dickerson's, and he just didn't look like the Randy I knew." That was God's appointment. And I knew it. It was like God set me up.

I got together with my friends who weren't saved. We had all the peace paraphernalia, and we went to this Baptist church where my friend with the healing gift was preaching a revival. I talked to him, and my friends were giving him all this barroom theology, but I came under conviction. The next day I went to his house, and I repented. And I was starting to head back. I wish I could say that was the last of my wild carrying on, but it wasn't. It was hard to come back. I mean, I wanted to be back, but I now had some stuff that I was struggling with.

So, a few weeks later, I went to the youth pastor at the Baptist church, and gave him this hallucinogenic stuff, asking him to get rid of it. I said, "I don't want this anymore. I've been a hypocrite, and I want to come back." But I was a double hypocrite. I was getting stoned with my friends and pretending to be a happy sinner. In my heart, I didn't like what I was doing; I knew I was happier in the Lord's House, knew I was really lonely and missing God.

Healing and Grace Sustain Faith

The following Sunday I was in a terrible car accident and almost killed. I had severe spinal injuries, paralysis, digestive system problems and more. My jaw had to be set, and I had broken ribs, but the main thing was the spinal injury. They weren't even sure I'd be able to walk again.

My unsaved paternal grandmother was a nurse in the hospital where I was taken, and she said, "You are lucky to be alive." The car looked like an accordion.

Despite these incredible injuries, God healed me. And that healing is what kept me from losing my faith in college and seminary. Because I couldn't deny my own healing.

Healing was the anchor. I went to a very liberal college and seminary that didn't believe in a lot of the miracles that Jesus did. They just didn't believe in anything supernatural, and that almost destroyed me. But the healing I had experienced was undeniable. I knew God heals today, because He healed me.

Healing was my reality, no matter what. For awhile my liberal professors and friends talked me out of nature miracles, talked me out of the reality of the demonic. I basically became the protégé of the most liberal professor in the college. By the time I graduated, some of my friends were praying for my re-conversion. It wasn't because of sin, but just because my theology had gone so far to the left. By the time I graduated, I knew I wasn't fit for the ministry any more. I was so confused over what I had been taught. So in seminary I tried to find the most conservative professors.

All the way through my education, it was the gifts, it was the presence, it was the reality of my healing that kept me from losing my faith. Eleven from my church went to that same school. By the time we graduated, only two of us were left as believers. The rest had all fallen away from God because of the teaching of the Bible school. So, God's grace helped me not to lose my faith.

Grace Through Trials

During this time I married a woman from a violent home. My bride saw her dad take a shotgun and shoot a hole in the wall on both sides of her mother. She married to get out of the horrendousness of this home.

Within two weeks of our marriage, before the honeymoon was over, she had already drawn blood on me. It was violent. For three years, we went to marriage counseling every week.

Despite that, in the second year, I found her in the garage with another man. In the third year, another man's wife called me to say, "Will you get your wife to stop having an affair with my husband." My wife was paying for the hotel bills with bad checks that I didn't have enough money to cover, adding up to more than my salary for a year, which was less than $2,000.

So the summer after I graduated from college, before I went to seminary, I was getting a divorce. I put this on my application for Southern Seminary, but for some reason they didn't catch it. So, I was admitted, and I went to seminary, burying myself in the pain. Instead of alcohol, I buried my pain in studies—best grades I ever made. I was doing well in school, was one of the most popular young Baptist preachers and was even being groomed to be a pastor in one of the largest churches in our association.

But then I was called in to see the Dean because of my results on the Minnesota Multiphasic Personality Inventory. He said, "You know, your MMPI says that you ought to be on the verge of a nervous breakdown, but you don't look like you are. How do you explain it?" I said, "Well, I'm at the end of a really tough divorce. And I almost had a nervous breakdown a year ago, when I realized my marriage wasn't going to work."

The Dean said, "What do you think we're going to do?" I said my professor in college told me you can go to Southern Seminary if you've had a divorce; they've changed the rule.

The Dean said, "Not if you get a divorce while you're going here; it has to be before. And, besides, you'll have to go to a psychiatrist. We'll have to make sure you're stable enough to be a pastor. We need letters from your college professors and the churches."

At that time I was pastoring at a tiny church — 12 people, six in Sunday School and all over 60. In fact, the church had closed the doors, but they had an endowment, and they didn't want to lose it, so they needed to keep the doors open. I figured, if I was going to go through a divorce, this was the best place for me to be because there was hardly anybody here who would get hurt by what was happening to me. I had walked away from a very fast-growing church and gone to this dead church specifically to avoid hurting anyone else. So despite the divorce, the board at the small church voted unanimously to keep me as their pastor.

Then the Dean said to me, "You're a bright student. But you will never have a ministry. You will never have a church. Your future as a minister is over. We're telling you this for your own good. You should go to law school. You'll get out of law school at the same time you would have gotten out of seminary. Same amount of time, same amount of study. But don't waste our Southern Baptist money and your time, because your ministry is over."

Added to what the Dean said was the fact that others, including my own pastor, even though his daughter had gone through a bad divorce, wanted to take my ordination away. I knew this situation could cause a big split in the association. So I said, "Just leave me alone for a time, and I'll become a Methodist or an American Baptist. I'll leave the denomination. I don't want to split the association over this. So just give me time, and I'll leave, because I don't want to cause a problem for you."

What I didn't understand then, but I know now, is that when people are conceived illegitimately, they will struggle with rejection—it's the biggest issue of their lives. So, I had a wife who was unfaithful and rejected me; the seminary has just kicked me out; and my own pastor, who I respected so much, wanted to pull my ordination. I came to realize the line of argument I was hearing about divorce was also a line of judgment for every divorced couple, causing guilt and condemnation to come upon everybody that's had a breakdown come upon their marriage.

So, long story short, I got back in. Why would I go back when they didn't want me? I was mad. Anger rides on hurt. I was mad because I felt so rejected. I decided I didn't want to have anything to do with the church. But I liked to work with people, and I knew that to be a United States Army chaplain you had to have a seminary education. So that's why I went back, not to prepare to pastor a church. I didn't want to pastor anymore. I decided to be a chaplain in the army, so I wouldn't have to deal with church.

In my pain, I began to drink alcohol—a stupid thing to do, something I didn't do even when I was backslidden at 18, but that's what I did. At that time, I was renting one room from a couple, and I came in one night, mad and a little bit tipsy, and I saw this picture of Jesus on the wall. And I went into a vision—one of only three I've had in my lifetime.

In the vision, I saw my favorite professor from college standing on the sidewalk outside his office. He said, "Randy, do you love the church of Jesus Christ enough to serve her when she hurts you?" At that time, I was the most popular young preacher in the whole association, and I said, "Yes!" It's easy to say things when you haven't had the test yet.

But the reality is, I realized as I said that, that this was the guy I had respected because he had been so severely hurt in a church he had grown from 0 to 700 that kicked him out over the race issue in 1962 in Mississippi. So, I knew this vision was from God, and the message was clear.

I got on my knees and I prayed, "Lord, I was running and I was trying to deal with my pain, and I didn't want to have anything to do with church. But Lord, you called me to preach. And Lord, they may be right. I may never have that big First Baptist Church again. That's over. But if all I can do is pastor a small bi-vocational church in the country somewhere and pump gas on the side to make a living because they don't make enough in the church to make a living with, then I want to be faithful to do that. Please forgive me for what I've been doing." And that was the turning point... grace. When I was messing up, grace brought a vision.

Grace to Overcome

The law said an illegitimate child for 10 generations can't come into the assembly. My mother was illegitimate, and my dad was illegitimate, and I was illegitimate. Yet, I've stood before hundreds of thousands of people and preached the gospel, because the dispensation of the Kingdom is so much greater than the dispensation of the law.

Maybe you have struggled in your marriage. Maybe you have failed in your career. Maybe you were illegitimate. Maybe you have had problems with sexual purity. Maybe you've never really given your life to God. Or maybe you're a hypocrite.

God wants to touch you with His grace, wants to redeem you. If you want more of His grace, extend grace by forgiving those who hurt you. The worst thing you can do is not forgive those who hurt you. If you don't forgive, you stay hooked to them. If you don't forgive, the pain keeps going because you are rehashing, and when you are rehashing, all those pains and memories just keep coming back to you. But if you forgive, you get unhooked. You don't have to believe what other people have said, but believe what He said.

When I received the vision and repented of turning my back on the church, my thought was, "Lord, you called me. I just want to deal with this rightly." I didn't stay in the ministry because I thought one day I was going to be successful. I stayed in the ministry because He called me, and I experienced grace.

It's hard not to be gracious when you've needed so much grace yourself. It's hard not to be gracious when you've been hurt by those who have no grace. And you can say, "I don't want to hurt others."

Grace to the Least

With all the grace we have received, we should never be surprised when God gives grace to others. Yet I don't understand why sometimes people that you think ought to be healed don't get healed, and sometimes people that you think don't deserve to be healed, they're the ones that get healed. Once when I was ministering in Seattle, the first people who got healed on the first two nights were street people with the smell of alcohol on them. It's like the Lord was saying, "I'm teaching you something. You've become more religious than you think. You slowly have become more religious than you think. And the fact that you are surprised or even shocked that the first people I healed were unsaved sinners with alcohol on their breath proves that you have become more religious than you think."

A few years ago, I went to India with a guy named Dave McKay, a portrait photographer for the rich and famous. While we were there, he got in trouble and almost caused a riot. We were walking from the hotel in one of the poorest of poor towns in India. An old man with long white hair in traditional Indian dress was sitting in a ditch, being blown by flies.

The compassion of the Lord came upon Dave, and he went and got some water to give to this guy. And you would have thought he had committed a huge social crime. Literally, that simple act almost started a riot! We had to say, "He didn't know any better." What did he do wrong? He helped that man. Why was he in trouble? Because Indian society and religion is based on karma and not grace. Dave was messing with this guy's karma, his fate. The man was in the ditch because that was what he deserved in this life. That was his karma! Don't mess with his karma! But grace says, "This is a child of God, no matter how bad or how low, and we need to take him some water." Big difference!

I don't want karma. I don't want what I deserve. I want grace. I don't want to be reincarnated so I can climb a ladder with each new life until I finally get good enough to go to Nirvana, which is like being a drop lost in the ocean. I want to know who I am. I want to know who my kids are.

I want to have eternity with them. I want eternal life and the grace God promises us. Karma is not good. If I'd gotten karma, I might be a snail right now!

Limited Grace or Full Grace?

Some of us have enough faith in the grace of God to say, like the prodigal son that came home, "I'm no longer worthy to be called your son, just make me like one of your hired servants." That son had bunkhouse thinking. Bunkhouse thinking is when we say to ourselves, "I believe enough in God that He'll forgive me, take care of me, give me food and shelter, supply my needs. But I've messed up, so I can never have that intimacy of coming into the big house, out of the bunkhouse and enjoying closeness with God." And so the prodigals come back and give themselves to God, but they don't expect full grace because they don't feel they deserve it.

Some time ago, I was trying to lead a man to the Lord. He was in prison for murder, and he couldn't understand how God could forgive him for that. He said, "No, it can't be that easy. There's no justice in that. If all I have to do is ask God to forgive me, there's no justice in that." I said, "Oh, there is justice in it. It's not like God just winks His eye and says, 'I'll forgive you' because there would be no righteousness, justice or holiness in that. You see, he can do it because His own son died for your sin." Once he understood the connection between justice and grace, he came to the Lord.

Grace means even though we don't deserve it, God gives it to us anyway. Less than a year ago, I was praying for a 16-year-old girl who had tumors throughout her body. It was late at night, and she didn't feel any different while we were praying. But after we stopped praying for her and were just talking with her and her family, she said she was getting hot, and there was heat all over her. I said, "Oh, that's the Lord! There's anointing here to pray." The power of God was all over her, and I said, "You come back tomorrow night, and we'll pray into this some more. I mean, you could be totally healed, but come back, and we'll pray some more." But she didn't come back the next night. Instead her mother did, and when I asked her where her daughter was, she said, "She didn't feel worthy of receiving our prayer."

That is the language of law, not grace. "I don't deserve…" is law, not grace. "I can't be forgiven…" is more faith in your sin, than in God's mercy and grace.

His Grace is Sufficient

Let me make this clear: No matter what you have done, the one who prayed for the people who crucified Him said, "Father, forgive them for they know not what they do." He stands ready to forgive. Some say, "Well, I've backslidden 10 times." Well, you're way short of that 70 x 7! You've got 480 more to go! And that's just an illustration of completeness.

You say, "How can He love that much?" You may have a hard time understanding God's love because you may be the harshest judge on yourself.

Just recently I was talking to someone who said, "I can't feel God." This person was having a struggle, and I said, "Was your father affectionate toward you in a healthy way?" "No." Often our struggle is not with God. It is with how we conceive of God in our own father's image. If you haven't had a healthy relationship with your father, it's harder for you to relate to God.

That's why, for my wife it was easier to relate to God than it was for me. That's true even though her father was an alcoholic and died of cirrhosis of the liver. Despite his alcoholism, he was very loving and very affectionate. She could always crawl on his lap, and did even when she was in her late 20's. She was the apple of his eye. Even though she did not grow up in church, it's been much easier for her to believe in a Father who wants to bless her. It's great to be raised in church but that's no substitute for having a mother and father that kids can see the image of God in. I've seen kids raised in church whose fathers were strict and disciplinarian, not affectionate and unloving, not very generous. And it's hard for them to believe God can be so generous and so loving.

Forgiving Yourself

So I encourage you to get it into your head how gracious God is. He's not like your mom or your dad; He's much more. How can He be so forgiving? It's because He knows us — better than we know ourselves. Once I understood that I was predisposed to making bad decisions because of my illegitimacy and the way I grew up, I could be much more merciful towards myself. Then it hit me, "God understands everything about us."

He understands every subconscious drive I have that I don't understand. He understands every wound that you have. He understands every weakness. That doesn't take away your personal responsibility for what you do, but it helps explain why God can be so merciful. That's why it's written in the Bible, "Even when our hearts condemn us, God is greater than our hearts."

When I went through the divorce, for a few weeks there I made some very poor choices. And I committed one sin that I asked God to forgive me of almost every night for 10 years. Now, in my head, I know I am forgiven. I would pray a prayer like this, "God, I know I'm already forgiven. I know your truth and I've confessed it. I know I'm already forgiven, but God I still feel so guilty that I did that, it makes me feel better to tell you one more time. I'm still sorry." But I knew I was forgiven. The problem was I knew God had forgiven me, but I hadn't yet been able to forgive myself.

Abundant Grace

Some of us have entered the Kingdom by faith, and we believe we've been forgiven. We understand we are sinners saved by grace. And that's wonderful. But we're not going to have a whole lot of victory if we camp there. I really want you to understand that this grace that brings you out and causes you to be born again takes you to the door. When we repent of our rebellion against God and change the way we think—God's right and I'm wrong—we go through the door of regeneration. So, now I'm a sinner that was just saved by grace. But more than that has happened.

Not only does Jesus save us, but He takes the signet ring of the Father (which is like the American Express platinum), and He gives it to you. "Son, you've been a prodigal, and you want to stay out here in this bunkhouse? No way, Jose! You come in here with me! I want intimacy with you. I'm going to hug you. I'm going to kiss you. You see this ring? I don't want you to think of yourself as a prodigal son anymore. I'm never going to bring it up to you. I'm never going to embarrass you. You are forgiven and to prove you are forgiven, here's the American Express Unlimited credit card. Use it for anything you need, because you are restored."

Now if we just come through the door and say, "I'm forgiven," we'll live like paupers, spiritually. We need to realize we are more than forgiven—and that's by God's grace. It's grace that forgave me and put the ring back on my finger. Now, in the authority of my Father's name because of what Jesus did, I can make decrees.

I don't see myself focused with Christ on the Cross. I was there for awhile but then He took me down, and He suffered my rejection. He suffered, for us, separation from God. But He's now seated at the Father's right hand. And you know what? So am I, and so are you! From that place there is great authority that's been entrusted to you. Many people can believe God's good enough to forgive them here, but they can't believe in full restoration because they're still stuck in bunkhouse thinking. I am not just a sinner saved by grace. I was once a sinner saved by grace!

Sons and Daughters with Authority

I'm the son of the Most High. I'm seated with Christ in heavenly places. All authority and power has been given to me and to you, and we have been instructed to use it on His behalf.

How do you know that you have come to understand grace in its fullness? Can you really see yourself on the throne, seated with Christ? God's grace for you doesn't stop with the door of regeneration. Yes, that's necessary, but that's not the end.

Jesus didn't die on the cross so you could be forgiven. Forgiveness was already available through the sacrificial system. And the New Covenant wasn't about forgiveness. The New Covenant promised that God would write His law on your heart. He would put His Spirit in you. The New Covenant is about the Spirit's relationship to you through grace. Under this covenant, God promises to set you in a place where sin can no longer corrupt you, but the spirit of God in you is greater than the sin in those who don't know Him.

This means you can walk right into the taverns now and begin to prophesy, and you can go where the parties are. Of course, if you've just come out of that, then maybe you should stay out of it for awhile. But as you grow, you get to a point where you can go in there, and you can make friends, and you can tell them what the Lord is like. The holiness in you can be stronger than the sin in them. Because He that is in you is greater than he that is in the world.

I really believe that if we could get a full understanding of grace, we would not need to go through most of the issues that we face as Christians. If we could get grounded in throne life at the beginning of our Christian life, we could walk in victory a lot more. Too often, as Bill Johnson says, we've repented—changed the way we think—enough to get into the Kingdom, but not enough to see the power of the Kingdom.

Don't stop at the doorway. He loves you. You and I don't understand how much He loves us. No matter what you've done, He's ready to forgive.

You may be struggling with whether or not you're good enough to get into the throne room. Or you may not be able to feel, to know in your heart, how deeply He has forgiven you. And, some of us have a smile on the outside when we're dying on the inside. Our issue is we have been judged so much by a critical father or a critical church we feel undeserving of grace. Yes, we can do things that bring consequences, and there is going to be a judgment, but we are to be ambassadors of reconciliation. And the Father has done all that is necessary for us to experience this total reconciliation. Total, not partial. Total reconciliation with God, with all shame and all guilt removed.

The Lord says to us, "My desire is not that you come out of the world through the door of regeneration, being born again. I want that for you, but son and daughter, I want you to draw so close that I can speak to you, and you can hear me, and you know who you are, and you are not afraid. And you know the authority that you have. I want you to think well of yourself. I want you to know that when I look at you, I don't see your imperfections. I see my Son's perfection. So, come close that you may obtain help and mercy in your time of need."

Grace. You start with it. You walk in it. And you end in it.

{ Out of the Bunkhouse }

One of my favorite illustrations comes from a preacher named Bob Harrington, known as the Chaplain of Bourbon Street. He was called to reach out to people on Bourbon Street in New Orleans, going into the highways and the byways as Jesus taught in the parable about the wedding feast. One evening as Bob was driving across that long bridge that crosses Lake Pontchartrain, he saw in the distance some fanatical guy. This crazy person was out of his car, standing in the road and waving his arms wildly.

Bob was tired, it was after midnight, and he thought, "Oh, my gosh. There is a prison over there, and maybe this guy is an escaped prisoner, and he is going to try and flag me down. Then he is going to kill me." And as he got closer, he could see the man more clearly. Bob swerved into the other lane to avoid him, but the crazy guy then jumped into that lane—still waving his arms madly. As Bob closed in on him, he realized the guy was yelling, "STOP! STOP! STOP! STOP!" Bob didn't want to stop because he was afraid of this wild man. Who knew what he might do? Finally, he rolled down the window to hear him more clearly and prepared to drive around him when he heard the whole message. The crazy man yelled, "STOP! The bridge is out! The bridge is out! A bus has already gone over the end!"

Then Bob slammed on his brakes, realizing that just a few hundred yards away, the bridge had been knocked out by a ship that had gone through, and already some people had tumbled to their deaths. But this man had risked his life to stand there and yell at Bob to stop, to save him from sudden and certain death. And that's what Jesus has done for us. From a cross, the crucified Savior yells to each of us: "STOP! STOP! STOP!"

Stop and Turn Around

Before they crucified him, Jesus was preaching this: "Except you repent, you will all likewise perish (Lk 13:3 & 5). Repent! For the Kingdom of Heaven is at hand. Repent! Turn from the direction you are going."

In modern America, we have denied the reality of hell and judgment. Christians know there will be a Great Judgment at the end of time, but God also judges in the present. His moral law is unchangeable. Everything we do has consequences. Believing parents, especially fathers, provide an umbrella, a covering over their families. When you yield to sin, you punch a hole in that covering. You allow a spirit to come in and attack your family, your sons and daughters in that area. Even if you don't care about going to hell, the devil will make sure that you can have hell in this life—both you and your children.

No Way But the Cross

Before He was betrayed, Jesus knew that He was about to be crucified. In the garden He cried out, "MY GOD! MY GOD! Father! If there is any other way, let this cup pass from me." The cup stood for God's wrath. For what? For sin. The cup was God's holiness saying, "I must judge sin.

I am a holy God. I must judge sin because I have said, "The soul that sins must die."

Jesus was crying out to the Father for another way, asking for the cup of God's wrath to pass from him. Luke's gospel tells us that He had prayed so desperately that his sweat was like drops of blood, drops of blood pouring out (Lk 22:44). He was asking God if there was any other way that you and Randy Clark could be forgiven, receive eternal life, go to heaven and be a part of the Kingdom of God on earth. Was there any other way besides Jesus' going to the cross?

Jesus was saying, "Oh, God. If they could just get baptized or circumcised, if they could just be catechized or confirmed, if there is any other way. Oh, God. If they could come to you except through me, repenting of their own works and self-righteousness and giving up their own trust in their own abilities and coming as poor and blind and as a beggar and saying, 'I have no hope except in your Son.' God, if there is any other way, if there is any other religion, if there is a morality, if there is a philosophy; if there is any other way that this could happen, don't let me have to go to the cross."

But there was no other way. And if Jesus couldn't convince the Father to provide another basis to let you in, I don't think you can either!

Jesus said, "I am the door, and no one comes to the Father but through me" (Jn 10:7 & 9; 14:6). If you try to come in any other way, you are the same as a thief and a robber. The way to God's heart is through repentance and faith in Christ Jesus. Now, that's just hard.

Mercy and Blessing to the Generations

God is holy, but God is also merciful. He tells us that a father's sin is visited upon the children to the second or third generation. But He said that for those that are righteous, there is blessing to a thousand generations.

I know people who have been sovereignly arrested by the Holy Spirit. Their mom and dad were as mean as could be. They were lost, didn't know the Lord, had never been in church and knew nothing of God. Still, the first time they heard the good news, the Spirit of God apprehended them. Later, I found out that somewhere in their heritage, there was a great grandmother or a grandfather who had been righteous, and that ancestor made a covenant.

God makes covenant with righteous people. Even if your children resist and harden their hearts and go out and become prodigals and never come back, God will still move upon your seed, upon your generations. He says, "I will touch them, I will come to them, I will draw them. Yes, they can resist me, but I will draw them and give them the opportunity because of your righteousness."

When you give your heart to the Lord, you open up a channel of blessing throughout a thousand generations to your seed. That's inheritance. Proverbs 22:13 says, "A good man leaves an inheritance for his children's children."

Receiving the Holy Spirit

Jesus purchased an inheritance for us, but you may have never been to the Father's House to claim it. You may have never known what it is like to feel the love of God. You have never known what it is like to have the Spirit of God come along beside you. In Greek, the word for Holy Spirit is *parakletos*, which means Comforter, Counselor, Guide or Helper. It literally means He who comes along beside you to help you in your time of need.

You are not here alone. That is why Jesus said it would be to our advantage for him to go away because then the Father would send the Holy Spirit. And the Apostle Paul said that the only way that you could really know that you are a Christian—in other words, the evidence, the guarantee, the down payment that you have eternal life—is receiving the Spirit.

Now, I want to suggest something. Do you believe that Jesus is the Son of God? Yes. The Bible says if you confess your sin, He will forgive you. Did you confess? Yes. Then, based on what the scripture says, you can know you are forgiven. That's logical assurance.

But let's look at this more closely. In 2 Corinthians 7:10, we read, "Godly sorrow brings repentance that leads to salvation and leaves no regret, but worldly sorrow brings death." The truth is, even the demons believe and tremble. Paul said the way that you can know that you are really born again, the way you can know that you are really a child of God, the way you can really know that you are a covenant person is that you have experienced the Spirit in your life.

When you receive the Spirit, the guilt lifts and His peace comes. You feel His love. If I had lived in the 1700s, I know I would have been a Methodist, with their experiential salvation. You don't have to leave it to guesswork because so many people have had false conversions. They have religion, but they don't have relationship with the Lord.

The Father's House

I want to tell you if you have never been in the Father's House, it is a wonderful place, and He loves to play with his kids. He doesn't get offended by laughing. When my children were small and I would return home after a trip, sometimes after two or three weeks, I would pull in the garage and hear those little voices and those feet running to the garage door, and they were saying, "Daddy's Home!!! Daddy's Home!!! Daddy's Home!!! Daddy's Home!!!" And I opened the door, and there they stood. They would raise their hands—not in worship—but because they wanted me to pick them up! They wanted me to hold them.

The Father's House is a place where children can be held—in the living room, in the family room. I used to love to get down and blow on my children's bellies and make those weird sounds and tickle them. Now I do it with my grandson. There is nothing I enjoy more than seeing my kids full of joy. And my hobby is to spend my life when I am home to make them and my wife happy. That brings the greatest happiness to me.

I don't want a servant. I could buy, I could hire, I could rent servants. I want children who know their father's love and who are not afraid to come to me.

Some of you have never known God that way, as a Father. You have never felt Him and never experienced His nearness. Some of you did and fell into sin, and you have come back, but your guilt is so bad, you don't feel like you could ever be used again. You don't think you are worthy to come into the living room. You feel that you are not worthy. You feel that you don't deserve to sit in the family room and let Him play with you anymore, to sit at the dining table and share with Him your dreams and interests and have intimate time with Father.

Staying in the Bunkhouse

Instead you have fallen into a trap of the enemy, and he has convinced you that though you are forgiven, you are no longer worthy to be in the Father's presence in the big house. You are forgiven and you know it, but you have relegated yourself to the bunkhouse, the migrant shack where the servants live, but not the children. And you have decided that it is just good enough to be a servant, to have just food and clothes, to be cared for by God because you know God will take care of his servants.

But the Father is saying, "Don't you know that is a trap of the enemy?" He doesn't want His children living like servants. He wants His children to serve Him because they love Him, but they are not to have a servant mentality. That's what I call "bunkhouse thinking."

Today in the Church, we have not understood the mercy and the grace of God. Sometimes we have not understood His wrath, and we have behaved without any fear of God. The other side of that is failing to understand his mercy and his love.

God's Grace

In Luke 15, we read that tax collectors and sinners gathered to hear Jesus, but the Pharisees and teachers of the law weren't pleased. In Luke 15:2, they said, "This man welcomes sinners and eats with them." We have a problem: Jesus liked sinners. You see, that is who He came to die for. It's the sick who need a physician, not the healthy.

Then Jesus told the parables of the lost sheep and the lost coin. Those who lost them looked and looked until they found them. Once they're found, there was a great celebration. These parables explain Jesus' heart for sinners.

But there is one more parable in Luke 15—one that almost everyone knows. You may have heard a thousand sermons on it. It's the parable of the Prodigal Son. But I think that's the wrong title. Because the son isn't really the emphasis of this story. The emphasis is the father. I would have called it the parable of the father who had two screw-up sons.

This is a story that shows us through this father what God is like. Luke 15:11-32 tells us:

> *The Parable of the Lost Son*
>
> *Jesus continued: "There was a man who had two sons. The younger one said to his father, 'Father, give me my share of the estate.' So he divided his property between them."*
>
> *"Not long after that, the younger son got together all he had, set off for a distant country and there squandered his wealth in wild living. After he had spent everything, there was a severe famine in that whole country, and he began to be in need. So he went and hired himself out to a citizen of that country, who sent him to his fields to feed pigs. He longed to fill his stomach with the pods that the pigs were eating, but no one gave him anything."*

"When he came to his senses, he said, 'How many of my father's hired men have food to spare, and here I am starving to death! I will set out and go back to my father and say to him: Father, I have sinned against heaven and against you. I am no longer worthy to be called your son; make me like one of your hired men.' So he got up and went to his father."

"But while he was still a long way off, his father saw him and was filled with compassion for him; he ran to his son, threw his arms around him and kissed him."

"The son said to him, 'Father, I have sinned against heaven and against you. I am no longer worthy to be called your son.'"

"But the father said to his servants, 'Quick! Bring the best robe and put it on him. Put a ring on his finger and sandals on his feet. Bring the fattened calf and kill it. Let's have a feast and celebrate. For this son of mine was dead and is alive again; he was lost and is found.' So they began to celebrate."

"Meanwhile, the older son was in the field. When he came near the house, he heard music and dancing. So he called one of the servants and asked him what was going on. 'Your brother has come,' he replied, 'and your father has killed the fattened calf because he has him back safe and sound.'"

"The older brother became angry and refused to go in. So his father went out and pleaded with him. But he answered his father, 'Look! All these years I've been slaving for you and never disobeyed your orders. Yet you never gave me even a young goat so I could celebrate with my friends. But when this son of yours who has squandered your property with prostitutes comes home, you kill the fattened calf for him!'"

"'My son,' the father said, 'you are always with me, and everything I have is yours. But we had to celebrate and be glad, because this brother of yours was dead and is alive again; he was lost and is found.'"

My prayer for you as you think about this story is that you would be so broken by the Father's love, so drawn by the Holy Spirit, that you cannot control the tears. I pray that you won't even try. I pray that you will say, "God, if you would just touch me, if I could just feel you, I would not wipe the tears away. I will not try to hold back the emotion." I pray that God will give you a new and far deeper revelation of his great grace.

Cultural Context

Now, let's look at this parable and see what Jesus was saying. I want us to try to see it through the ear and the eye of the first-century Jewish person. I think we receive more that way. There are some things that we Gentiles won't understand unless we can get back into that context. We must remember that Jesus was a Jew, and all of his first disciples were Jews.

Almost all of the New Testament was written by them.
First of all this man, the father, had two sons, and he was
going to divide up his living. Here's the interesting thing—
when do you receive an inheritance? The fact that this boy
was asking his father for his share of the inheritance is the
same as him saying, "Dad, I can't wait for you to die." He
shamed his father. He didn't want to wait.

Despite this, the Bible says the father divided his estate
between them. What did the younger son get? This is where
we need to understand the Jewish culture. In that culture,
the first born got a double portion. So, what did the Prodigal
Son get? A third. And the older son got two-thirds. Keep
that in mind.

So the young boy went off and had a party, traveled to the far
country and left his father's presence. He thought it wasn't
good at home; he could have more fun out on his own. He
went the way that many do, and he spent all of his money in
wild living and riotous living, on wine, women and song—
on partying and cocaine. When he ran out of money, oddly
enough, he ran out of friends. When he ran out of money to
throw the party, his friends had gone, too. He found himself
all alone.

At that point, as Jesus told the story, the boy wound up going
to a farmer and feeding pigs. We Gentiles don't understand
that. We need to remember that swine are unclean to Jewish
people. The fact that this young man would find himself in
the midst of swine and eating what they eat would have been
unthinkable to the people Jesus was speaking to.

A Modern-Day Prodigal

If our Lord came today and told this story, He would say a young man had a rich father, and he asked his father for his inheritance. His father gave it to him, and he went to Chicago, and he went to Washington, D.C., and he got hung up and strung out on crack cocaine. He threw parties, and he went to the best nightclubs. He traveled by stretch limousine, and he had the girls and everything he wanted, and then he ran out of money. The habit got hold of him, and he couldn't control it, and he went through the whole inheritance.

Then the boy found himself on the streets of Washington, D.C., or Baltimore, huddled over a steam grate covered by a box. He was going through garbage cans for food, living on the street, on skid row. And then he came to himself. That's how Jesus would tell the story today.

This lost son came to himself and said, "How many of my father's hired men have food to eat, and here I am starving to death? I will arise and I will go back to my father and say, 'Father, I am no longer worthy to be called your son.'"

All Unworthy

Now, let's pause here and think about this. Had this boy been living in a way worthy of his father's name? No way. So when he said, "I am no longer worthy to be called your son," that was true. He was unworthy. Just as we are unworthy, all of us.

It's important to understand that we are sinners. Only when we understand just how unworthy we are, how much we need forgiveness can we appreciate God's forgiveness. Only a drowning person appreciates a lifesaver. Only someone who's lost or backslidden, like I was at 18—in the church or not—understands what it means to be unworthy. When I was 18, I wasn't worthy to be called by my Father's name. I was at church three times a week and stoned every night. For ten months I took Jesus' name and brought shame to it.

The son in Jesus' story decided to go home, and he knew what he was going to say. He was going to say, "I am no longer worthy to be called your son; make me like one of your hired men."

Let me switch for a minute to the other son, the older brother. I have a theory about him. I think that the older son had created a model of what life was like with the father. The older son didn't understand his father's love, and he lived way beneath his privileges. But he was a really hard worker, and the younger boy said, "I don't want to live like that, just working all the time. I want to go and have some fun."

Some people look at the church and see no joy, no peace, no love. All they see is service. Now there is nothing wrong with service. Lovers do serve each other. But if we are just focused on service to meet requirements of religion, then we're in servitude. Without knowing the Father and his love, we've got it backward. We're serving to gain acceptance. But God offers us acceptance, and then out of gratefulness we want to serve.

Enemy Strategies

The younger boy didn't understand the difference. So he ran off. When he got ready to come back, the enemy had a strategy to keep the distance between him and his father. The enemy employs two opposing strategies to separate us from God. If one won't work, maybe the other will. First, he wants you to believe that you are so good that you don't need to be forgiven, and so you don't need Jesus. Second, he'll try to convince you that you are so bad that God won't forgive you.

Those are the two strategies of Satan. You are so good, you are so moral, you are as good as any of the people in the church. Well, that may be true. You may be better than some, and maybe better than most morally. But nobody is going to heaven because they are moral. Nobody will go to heaven because they are a good neighbor, a good husband or a good father. Hell is full of good moral people.

In Isaiah 64:6, we read, "All of us have become like one who is unclean, and all our righteous acts are like filthy rags; we all shrivel up like a leaf, and like the wind our sins sweep us away." The word translated here as "filthy rags" actually means "menstrual cloth." And Isaiah chose it purposely. He said no matter how good our deeds are, they don't make us right with God, they don't get us to heaven. Our righteousness is nothing compared to the righteousness of Jesus Christ. In Romans 3:23, Paul put it this way, "for all have sinned and fall short of the glory of God."

The younger son recognized he had sinned, and he was ready to go home and confess that he was no longer worthy to be called a son, and he simply wanted to be a hired servant. That is the enemy's strategy. But God has a different strategy. When you come to the Father, He doesn't want you to be a servant. He has angels to serve him. He wants you to be a son or a daughter. Yes, as you love him, you will serve him.

But what He really wants is your heart, not your service. It's not your money either. Tithing won't get you to heaven. God doesn't care about your piddley little tithe. His streets are gold and his gates are pearl. What does He need? He is not in need of money. You can't buy your way in. You don't get in because Dad and Mama are Christians. So the enemy came to the younger son, saying, "Just be a servant."

Seeing Each Other

The boy headed for home, and on his way, he saw his father. His father saw him. The scripture says the father saw his son and had compassion on him. That's interesting. Normally, older men's vision gets dimmer, and younger men's vision is clear. The son and the father were equal distance from each other when they saw each other.

I believe the son was looking for the father. The scripture says that the father looked down (maybe it was a dirt road) and saw his son, and what a joy leapt up in him. What a love he felt. Here again is another cultural difference that we can easily miss. It's important for us to know that the elders of the city never ran in public. It was a shameful thing for a man of distinction to be seen running, but Jesus said this father ran to his son. He threw caution and decorum to the wind, what anybody else thought to the wind. He didn't care. This father was so in love with his son, even though he had sinned against him, that he ran to greet him.

And Jesus was saying to the Pharisees, "That's why I am out here with the sinners—that's why. You must understand why I am telling you this parable, why I've come to die. I love sinners! I have come to rescue them."

The scripture says, the father ran. I think the boy was surprised. He really didn't know the depth of his father's love. And the father threw his arms around his son and hugged him and kissed him. Do you think the boy felt awkward?

God is Calling Now

You may feel awkward, too, as you realize how much God loves you. He is running to you. You don't feel worthy. You know you have been out there messing around, and you have taken his name into the gutter. You know you are not worthy. But that doesn't stop God. He is coming to you! He is coming to you! Do you feel his love? Do you feel him drawing your heart? God is running to you, calling you to himself.

We can only come to God and get saved, when He draws us. You can't decide two years from now would be a better time. I will finish this affair, and then two years from now I will get right with God. Two years from now, He may not be drawing you and your heart may be hardened. And your season and the opportunity and the sovereign purposes of God may have ended.

God comes knocking on His time, not yours. So, if you are surprised with the presence of God touching you as you read this, just think about it. The God that created the universe is touching you and giving you an invitation to be converted right now. The Father's arms may be around you right now.

Are you going to wiggle out of his arms and say NO to him? Or are you going to receive your wedding raiment, because you have to be clothed in his garment. The enemy may be whispering to you and raising guilt in your mind, telling you that you don't deserve God's love. That's what the son in Jesus' story thought. He said to his father, "Father, I have sinned against heaven and against you! I am no longer worthy to be called your son."

Grace Instead of Justice

As he was sitting with the pigs, deciding what to do, I believe the boy remembered what his father was like. I think he said to himself, "My father is a good and just man. He is a moral man. If a man works hard, he will pay him a day's wages." This wayward son believed in the justice of his father, and many of us also believe in the justice of God. If there is a God, we reason, He must be just.

I believe that's true. But when this son came home, he experienced far more than the justice of God. He experienced the grace of God when his father threw his arms around him. He was looking for justice and got grace when he was willing to repent.

If we got justice, we would get hell. Isaiah 53:6 tells us, "We all, like sheep, have gone astray, each of us has turned to his own way; and the Lord has laid on him the iniquity of us all." There is none righteous, no not one, the scripture says. So we don't want justice. We want grace.

What the son told the father was true—I am no longer worthy to be called your son. But the father did a miraculous thing. He said to his son, "Here is my VISA card, and here are the keys to the car, and I am ordering a caterer to throw a big party for you." Now, the ring he gave his son was like the VISA card. The father said, "And man, get out of those stinking clothes! We are going to get you some nice clothes because you are my son."

God's Grace for You

Maybe you'd like to change clothes, too. Would you like to take off the clothes of shame, hopelessness, fear of death, emptiness and meaninglessness? Would you rather be clothed with the righteousness of Christ and wear hope, love and peace?

Think about this. If you are lost, this is the picture God has for you. If you are backslidden or never truly saved, this is the picture for you. God waits for you and He runs to you, but it's still your choice. You can run away.

You can harden your heart and try to control your will and try to control your emotions and say "I am not going to cry. I am not going to do this. I don't want to do this. I have got plans for my life."

Or you could say, "I am not going to run. I am not going to turn away from God. I am going to run into your arms, God."

The Older Brother

Let's look back at the story. Some years ago, God gave me a deeper insight into the wealth of the Father's love. And it's about the older son. While the father was out running to meet his younger son, the older son was in the field. He heard music and dancing, and he asked the servant what was going on. The servant said, "Your brother was lost and he has been found and your father is throwing a party." "Now," the father said, "we have got to celebrate."

When the Holy Spirit fell in Toronto in 1994, I said, "God, what is all the laughing about? God, this is kind of weird. There are people getting drunk." He said, "Son, I had to throw a party! The prodigals are about to come home. I am getting ready to have a harvest, and I am getting the Church ready so it is not a mortuary and it is not a funeral parlor. It is a party atmosphere because angels in heaven rejoice when one sinner repents. When a bunch of my sons and daughters are coming back to me, there has to be joy in my house. No longer do I want the Church to be the most boring place on Sunday morning or Saturday night. I want it to be the most exciting place. I want there to be JOY in my house. I want there to be LOVE in my house. And so I am changing the atmosphere in my house because I know in my sovereign purposes that revival is coming, and the prodigals are coming back."

But the older brother wasn't happy about the party, and he wouldn't go in. This is what I want you to hear. God LOVES the whole Church from the bells and the smells and the candles and the incense to the Holy Rollers. The Church is his family. It is his Church and He LOVES the whole Church, and He is throwing a party. Revival is God's party. Revival is for all of us.

Sometimes those who have labored before in the past aren't always pleased when Father throws his party. Now, this older son has a problem. He is jealous, and jealousy gets in the Church at large. One denomination is jealous of another. We have a tendency to say, "God didn't throw his party for me, and I'm not going to yours."

But we need to understand this: the party was to celebrate the son coming home, but it was the father's party for all his people. But the older son's attitude was, "Well, I don't like parties. I would rather work. I am uncomfortable at parties. I don't like to play. I don't like all that mushy stuff." You see, the older boy had a problem.

Two Prodigals

Here's the truth I want you to grasp: this father didn't have one prodigal son. He had two. He had one who didn't want a relationship with his father; he wanted to do his own thing. And he had another son whom the enemy had taken not into degradation but into religion.

The devil had tried to tell the younger boy who was coming back to his father, "Just tell him you are no longer worthy to be called his son; you will be his servant." But here's the reality: a servant is exactly what the older boy had become. He, too, had bunkhouse thinking. That's why he was mad.

The father went out to the older son and pleaded for him. He wanted his family to be complete. And yet, the younger son is oblivious to the fact that his older brother is not there. He is partying up in God's presence while his brother is still outside.

The Father's Heart

We need the whole family of God to be complete—not just the Charismatics and Pentecostals, but all the Church needs to be part of revival. I am telling you, I have heard the Father's heart, and the Father's heart is not just for the Charismatics and the Pentecostals. The Father's heart is for the whole Church to be revived, to get out of the bunkhouse, to know him personally, to have relationship. It is for the whole Church. If you look into the history of older denominations, you can find where they have been wooed and loved on, but sometimes we forget that.

The father in Jesus' story went out to the older son. He pleaded. He begged him to come in to the party. But listen to what the son said. He answered his father, "Look, all these years I have been slaving for you." What does that suggest?

If you are a wife, how would you feel if your husband came home and said, "Honey, I have been slaving for you for 22 years, for 37 years, for 40 years."? Would you feel loved? No! You would feel offended. Why? Because LOVE does not count service as slavery. LOVE counts service as privilege. LOVE likes to serve the beloved, and you don't use the word slaving for the service that is from the heart to the beloved.

Out of the Bunkhouse

It's time to come out of the bunkhouse. If you are in a bunkhouse relationship with God, it's time to come out. Let him LOVE you. If your answer to the Father is the same as the older son's, "Look, all these years I have been slaving with you and never disobeyed your orders," you're caught in legalism.

Do you say, "Oh! I have never! I have never had a drink of whiskey in my life. I have never been to a peep show, never been to a movie, never been to a dance." Every group has its own list of dos and don'ts. If you've followed the rules, never disobeyed orders, that's legalism. It is law; it is religion.

LOVE says, "Tell me what makes you happy. Tell me what pleases you. Tell me because you have saved my soul from hell, and you have touched me with your love. I want to respond and love you."

I wasn't raised amongst educated people. I was raised in

some pretty rough places, in one of the 50 poorest counties in the United States. My mother is one of two people in the whole village who had a high school education. Most of them had an eighth grade education or less. We just didn't handle discipline appropriately. We had hickory switches and belts and paddles. Some fathers were worse than that, and you were careful in how you smart-mouthed your father because some of them would use you as a mop across the floor.

Because of how I was raised, I have always been amazed at the smart mouth of this older son here. He is smart-mouthing his father. In my mind, he deserved some of that old-fashioned discipline. But, you see, the younger son didn't get what he deserved, and this older son didn't get what he deserved either.

Why? Because the father loved his children—both of them. This older son even starts accusing his brother. I hate it when my kids cut each other down. The Father doesn't like it when we cut each other down. I mean, the Father wants us to build each other up. Isn't it a sign of dysfunction in a home when they are cutting each other down and speaking badly about each other instead of encouraging and enriching? We call that a dysfunctional family.

God doesn't want us to be dysfunctional. He doesn't. Boy! He got all over my case about talking about a part of the family that I didn't like. He got all over my case about a part of the family that I differed with. The Church has got to quit being dysfunctional. We have got to quit cutting each other down. We need to start building each other up.

You might think, "Well, I am not the prodigal." I first started preaching this sermon when I was 18 years old. I had just come out of sin. I had just gotten out of drugs. I identified with the boy—the young one. I identified with the prodigal. When I would preach it, I could feel for him and the father's love for him.

But it has been 27 years since then, and I have been walking with God. Now, my danger is that I am the older brother. I have walked in his shoes and I have cut down my younger brother somewhere. What has got my heart now is the LOVE, the father's love, for the older brother.

The father's love for the older brother is for any local church, in any of the historic denominations. He will go after them, and the enemy will try keep them from coming to the party.

Listen to what this father said. He said, "My son." He didn't say, "Young man, listen to me!" He said, "My son"—a term of endearment—"you are always with me." Look at this. I never saw this before. The father said, "Everything I have is yours."

Do you know what the problem was? The father killed the older boy's goat. Was he feeling protective? Jealous? What happens when we have a great revival? Maybe you have 2,000 Gen X'ers with spiked hair and purple hair and pants hanging down to the middle of the rump start showing up—coming to a building they never paid for, sitting in the seat where you've always sat, taking your parking space. The danger we will face is becoming the older brother.

God Seeks Us Because of Love

What we must do is never lose sight of this: what's

happening is not about the older brother or the younger son. Revival is about the father and his love for his children. It's about dancing and laughing, a party atmosphere because our Father said to party. God doesn't want any of us to perish. He wants everyone to repent and come to everlasting life.

We all know John 3:16, "For God so loved the world that he gave his one and only Son, that whoever believes in him shall not perish but have eternal life." Jesus said, "Father, if there is any other way, let the cup of your wrath pass from me." But there wasn't any other way. So don't try to offer any other way except the cross, except Jesus where you come and say, "Lord, I have no faith in my morality, no confidence in me, I plead guilty and ask for mercy because of what Jesus did."

God offers us forgiveness. There's nothing you have done that He won't forgive. He loves you. He wants a relationship with you whether you've never come to him before, whether you're a returning prodigal or whether you're a hypocrite with a double life.

My prayer for you is that God would open your eyes and soften your heart so that you can come to him. I pray that He will draw you with his love.

Coming to God is as simple as ABC. A, you need to Acknowledge you are lost. You need a savior. You need to acknowledge you are a sinner and need a savior. B, you need to Believe. You need to believe that Jesus is the Son of God who died for your sins, and believe that if you will repent, He will forgive you. Have faith that if you ask God to forgive you because of what Jesus did, He will. C, you need then to act on that faith, act on that belief, Confess your sins, and commit your life to be his son or his daughter. If you will do A, B and C, God will do D. He will Deliver you from damnation, and He will Deliver you from the oppression in your life. That's how simple it is.

Prayer of Commitment

Lord Jesus, I invite you into my heart and my life. I know I am a sinner, that I am lost without you. Forgive me for the things I've done wrong. [Take time to tell him specifically the things you know you've done.] I know that you are the Son of God, who died for my sins. I yield my life to you, and I accept your forgiveness and love. Please come into my life by your Holy Spirit to be with me forever. Thank you, Lord Jesus. Amen

Other books by Randy Clark

Entertaining Angels

There Is More

Power, Holiness and Evangelism

Lighting Fires

God Can Use Little Ole Me

Changed in a Moment

Other Booklets by Randy Clark

Evangelism Unleashed

*Learning to Minister Under the Anointing /
Healing Ministry in Your Church*

Training Manuals Available

Ministry Team Training Manual

Schools of Healing and Impartation Workbooks

Core Message Series

Words of Knowledge

Biblical Basis of Healing

Baptism in the Holy Spirit

Open Heaven

Pressing In

The Thrill of Victory / The Agony of Defeat

Awed By His Grace / Out of the Bunkhouse

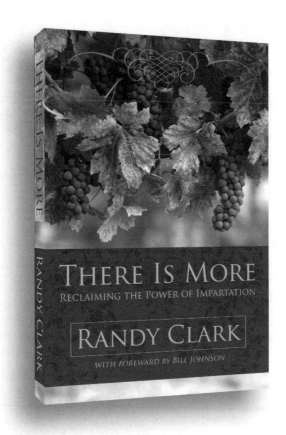

In "There Is More", Randy lays a solid biblical foundation for a theology of impartation as well as taking a historical look at impartation and visitation of the Lord in the Church. This is combined with many personal testimonies of people who have received an impartation throughout the world and what the lasting fruit has been in their lives. You are taken on journey throughout the world to see for yourself the lasting fruit that is taking place in the harvest field - particularly in Mozambique. This release of power is not only about phenomena of the Holy Spirit, it is about its ultimate effect on evangelism and missions. Your heart will be stirred for more as you read this book.

"This is the book that Randy Clark was born to write."

- Bill Johnson

Vision
To release followers of Christ into their specific destiny and calling, in order to live out the Great Commission.

Structure
Global School of Supernatural Ministry is a one or two year ministry school with an emphasis on impartation and equipping students for a life of walking in the supernatural. Classes start each September and end the following May. Courses are offered on-site at the Apostolic Resource Center in Mechanicsburg, PA. Upon completion of each program year a Certificate of Completion is awarded. Students seeking additional educational training may do so while attending GSSM through the Wagner Leadership Institute.

Community
The GSSM student body is diverse in age, culture, ministry experience, and educational accomplishments. From high school graduates to professionals to retirees - the students come together seeking more of God. Supernatural power, passion and honor are key values of GSSM and are reflected in our worship, outreach and personal relationships.

For more information - or to enroll in classes - contact us at
1-866-AWAKENING or apply online at
http://gssm.globalawakening.com

globalawakening

For a schedule of upcoming events and conferences, or to purchase other products from Global Awakening, please visit our website at:

http://www.globalawakening.com